OUR ANGRY PLANET

Forest Fires

ANNE ROONEY

Adapted from an original text by Anita Ganeri

FRANKLIN WATTS
LONDON•SYDNEY

First published in 2009 by Franklin Watts

Copyright © 2009 Arcturus Publishing Limited

Franklin Watts
338 Euston Road
London NW1 3BH

Franklin Watts Australia
Level 17/207 Kent Street, Sydney, NSW 2000

Produced by Arcturus Publishing Limited,
26/27 Bickels Yard, 151–153 Bermondsey Street, London SE1 3HA

Our Angry Planet is based on the series *Nature's Fury*, published by Franklin Watts.

Editor: Alex Woolf
Designer: Mind's Eye Design and Mike Reynolds

Picture Credits
Corbis: 4 (F Krahmer/zefa), 5 (Jim Sugar), 7 (T Allofs/zefa), 8 (Aim Patrice), 9 (Dr Vic
Bradbury), 10 (Tom Bean), 12 (Reuters), cover and 14 (J Emilio Flores), 15 (Frank Lane Picture
Agency), 16, 18 (Brian A Vikander), 20 (Parrot Pascal), 21 (Viviane Moos), 23 (Reuters), 24
(Aim Patrice), 25 (Yves Forestier), 26 (John Heseltine), 27 (T Allofs/zefa), 28 (Dale C Spartas),
29 (Raymond Gehman).
FLPA: 17 (Michael Quinton/Minden Pictures), 19 (Jim Brandenburg/Minden Pictures).
Mind's Eye Design: 6.
NASA Visible Earth: 11 (Jacques Descloitres, MODIS Land Rapid Response Team at NASA
GSFC), 22 (Image by Robert Simmon, based on data from NASA GSFC, MITI, ERSDAC, JAROS,
and US/Japan ASTER Science Team).
Science Photo Library: 13 (John Reader).
Shutterstock: cover (Arnold John Labrentz).

A CIP catalogue record for this book is available from the British Library.

Dewey Decimal Classification Number: 363.37'9

ISBN 978 0 7496 9048 9

Printed in China

Franklin Watts is a division of Hachette Children's Books, an Hachette UK Company
www.hachette.co.uk

Contents

What is a Forest Fire?   4

What is a Fire?   6

How Forest Fires Start   8

Human-Made Forest Fires   10

How Forest Fires Spread   12

Types of Forest Fire   14

Fire and the Landscape   16

Forest Recovery   18

Forest Fires and People   20

Fighting Forest Fires   22

Firefighting Equipment   24

Fire Warnings and Protection   26

Preventing Forest Fires   28

Ten of the Deadliest Forest Fires   30

Glossary   30

Further Information   31

Index   32

What is a **Forest Fire?**

Forest fires are terrifying and spectacular. Giant flames leap into the air and thick, black smoke rises in towering columns. The fires burn leaves and branches to a crisp, and dried-out trees explode into flames.

A fiery path

▼ Fire rages through a pine forest in Yosemite National Park in the USA.

A tiny spark can start a huge fire. If it lands on dry plants, the spark quickly grows, with flames spreading in all directions. Forest fires are also called wildfires. They kill trees and other

plants, even burning roots underground. People and animals caught near a fire may be killed by smoke. Firefighters do not try to stop large forest fires. Instead, they control them so that they cannot spread too far. The fire finally burns itself out. A blackened wasteland is left behind.

Where and why?

Fires are more common during **droughts**. Hot summer weather dries out plants. The dry vegetation burns easily and the fire spreads quickly. Fires burn all kinds of woodland and forest. They also burn grassland, **scrub** and moor. Most fires are started accidentally by people. Some are ignited by lightning.

A NATURAL CYCLE

Forest fires are part of a natural cycle. They clear the land and allow new plants and trees to grow. Some trees even need fires to give them the chance to grow. Forest fires have always happened. Layers of charcoal in rocks and blackened rings in old trees show us that fires happened long ago.

▲ These scientists are cutting a slice from a giant sequoia tree. The rings will show them when forest fires have happened.

What is a **Fire?**

Fire happens when a material burns. Burning is a chemical reaction. The burning material reacts with **oxygen**, a gas in the air. The material glows red-hot and there are often flames. The hot material and flames give off heat and produce smoke.

The fire triangle

A fire needs three things to keep burning. It needs something to burn – this is called fuel. It also needs oxygen and heat. These three things make up the fire triangle. The oxygen comes from the air, so fires need air. The fuel is anything that can burn, such as leaves and wood. There is more about fuels on pages 12–13. Heat is needed to start a fire. Once it is going, a fire makes its own heat.

Flames and smoke

Plant material, such as leaves and wood, is made of many substances. In a fire some of these

▼ The fire triangle shows the three things that are needed for a fire to burn.

substances break down. They give off gases that burn in the air, producing heat and light, which we see as flames. **Carbon** is left behind. It glows red-hot as it burns. Tiny bits of carbon float into the air and make smoke. Water boils from the plants, making steam.

◀ The bark of this tree glows as the carbon in it burns.

STOPPING FIRE

A fire can only burn if it has heat, fuel and oxygen. If one of these is taken away or runs out, the fire dies. Firefighters stop a fire by taking away the fuel, covering the fire so it has no air, or cooling it with water.

How **Forest Fires Start**

A fire can only start if the fuel is dry and there is a source of heat. The fuel is the wood and leaves on the forest floor.

Where fires happen

Fires are most common in places that have a cool, wet winter and a hot, dry summer. Plants and trees grow well in these conditions, so there is lots to burn. In the summer plants and trees are very dry, so they burn easily. There are thousands of fires each year in North America and south-east

▲ Firefighters battle a fire in the south of France in 2001. The fire started after a drought.

CASE STUDY

Fire in France

Summers are very hot and dry in the south of France. Forests dry out and hundreds of fires start each year. About every six years there is a major fire. Strong summer winds fan the flames, making the fires spread quickly.

Australia. If there is a severe **drought,** even a tropical rainforest can dry out and burn.

The fire season

Most fires happen during the summer. The time in the year when fires are mostly likely is called the fire season. Drought makes fires more likely because vegetation dries out. Droughts happen if seasonal rains do not come or if it is dry for months.

What starts fires?

Fires are started by natural events or by people. Lightning is the most common natural cause of fire. Lightning strikes the Earth 100,000 times a day. Sometimes a volcanic eruption causes a fire. Plants rotting on the forest floor can also start a fire. They produce heat as they rot.

▲ **Lightning sends electricity through a tree. This heats the tree very quickly and can make it burst into flames.**

Human-Made
Forest Fires

In the USA, four out of five forest fires are started by people. In Australia, nine out of ten fires are started by people. Most are started by accident, but some are deliberate.

▼ Campfires must be carefully controlled to stop a dangerous fire spreading.

Accidental fires

Many fires are started when campfires or rubbish fires get out of control, or when people do not put them out properly. Dropped cigarette butts and matches also cause fires. Sparks from trains and machinery can cause fires if they fall onto a dry forest floor.

Fire for land management

People have been lighting fires for 60,000 years. They used fire to clear land for farming and living on. This is called **slash-and-burn**. It is a common cause of forest fires. Land is often cleared by fire in the Amazon rainforest. During a **drought**, the fire can easily get out of control and cause a lot of damage.

Deliberate fires

Some fires are started on purpose without a good reason. About a quarter of the fires started by people in the USA are lit by vandals. Some people do it to burn down property. Others do it for the thrill of seeing a fire.

▲ This photo taken from space shows the island of Borneo in Indonesia. Each red dot is a forest fire. Most started from slash-and-burn fires.

CASE STUDY

Indonesian fires, 1997

People burn forests in Indonesia to clear land. In 1997 many fires got out of control because the forest was very dry. The fires burned for months until rain finally put them out. Smoke affected many cities in Malaysia, Singapore and Indonesia. Millions of people suffered breathing problems.

How **Forest Fires Spread**

▼ **This forest fire in Cyprus spread quickly uphill, fanned by high winds.**

Heat from a fire spreads in two ways. It spreads as rays of heat called **radiation**, and as hot air currents, called **convection**. The heat makes nearby fuel hot enough to catch fire. The fire burns with flames and smoke. The line of flames is called a flame front. It spreads through the forest.

Spreading factors

Fire spreads in different directions at different speeds. Fire spreads most quickly in the direction the wind is blowing. The wind brings fresh air, feeding the flames, so the fire burns quickly. Fire moves uphill more quickly than downhill. Hot air from the fire rises and dries out the fuel above, making it burn more easily.

Fuel for forest fires

The material that burns is called fuel. The needles, leaves and branches of trees are fuel. So are small trees and shrubs, grass, fallen leaves, needles and branches on the forest floor. Rotting leaves and logs and even underground roots also burn. Some types of fuel burn more quickly than others. Pine trees burn more quickly than **deciduous** trees (trees that lose their leaves in winter). Trees that contain a lot of oil, such as eucalyptus trees, burn quickly.

▲ Fire spreads quickly through dry grassland.

FIRE SPEED

In calm conditions a fire may creep through deciduous forest at only 0.5 kilometres per hour (about 15 centimetres a second). But it can move at eight kilometres an hour over grassland on a windy day – that's faster than walking pace.

Types of **Forest Fire**

A forest has three layers. All three can burn. The crown is the top layer, made of the leaves and branches of mature trees. The surface layer is the forest floor. The ground layer is below the surface.

Crown, surface and ground fires

Crown fires spread through the treetops. Flames leap between trees and the forest floor is untouched. Crown fires spread quickly, carried by strong winds. They are the fiercest forest fires.

▼ A crown fire spreads through treetops near Los Angeles in the USA in 2004.

Surface fires spread over the forest floor, burning forest **litter**, grass, shrubs and small trees. They are the most common forest fires. They often leave the crown untouched.

Ground fires burn underground, without flames. Buried and rotting litter and tree roots slowly smoulder. They can burn unseen.

Blow-ups and fire devils

Forest fires burn very fiercely through pine forests. The needles dry out and burn instantly. Hot air rises from the burning trees. It pulls in more air from the sides, fanning the flames. The **temperature** can be over 1,000 degrees Celsius and the flames hundreds of metres tall. These terrifying fires are called blow-ups. They can make burning whirlwinds called fire devils.

▲ A fire spreading over the surface and through the crown has burned these eucalyptus trees in Portugal.

CASE STUDY

Australian bush fires

South-east Australia has very hot, dry summers and dry winters. There are lots of eucalyptus trees, which burn easily. In 1983, ten months of **drought** ended in fierce forest fires. Strong winds blew trees onto power lines. The trees caught fire and the fires spread quickly. Some flames were 375 metres high. Seventy-one people died.

Fire and the Landscape

Surface fires kill young trees, but mature trees usually survive. Their thick bark protects them. However, if the bark is damaged, diseases or insects may get in and harm the tree. Crown fires often kill older trees. Many trees can lose up to a third of the crown and still survive. Ground fires kill old and young trees by burning their roots.

▼ Every tree in this forest has been damaged by a forest fire, but some may still be alive.

Changes to soil

Fire destroys **nutrients** in the soil that plants need. It also kills **micro-organisms** that break down rotting plants in soil. However, fires add ash to the soil. This has other nutrients, such as potassium, magnesium and calcium.

If rotting plant matter and roots are destroyed, there is nothing to hold the soil in place so it is easily washed away. Then there is no soil for new plants to grow in.

Effect on animals

Some animals are killed by smoke, but few are killed by flames. Most large animals can run away from fires, and birds can fly away.

▲ This elk in Yellowstone National Park is in more danger from the smoke than from the fire.

Small burrowing animals can hide underground. Insects and very tiny animals often cannot escape and are killed. Many animals lose their habitats in fires.

CASE STUDY

Yellowstone National Park, 1988

In 1988 a long period with no rain or snow dried out trees in Yellowstone National Park in north-western USA. Lightning started many fires. Firefighters let some burn. These quickly got out of control and burned an area of forest the size of 150,000 football pitches. Thousands of animals died.

Forest Recovery

Straight after a forest fire, the forest looks like a dead wasteland. However, within months, green shoots appear. Plants and animals return. After 20 years, all sign of the fire has gone. Forest fires have been happening for millions of years and the forests always recover.

Succession

The order in which plants and animals come back to the forest is called succession. The first plants are grasses and weeds. These are called pioneer plants. The ash in the soil helps them to grow. Some grow from seeds left in the soil. Others spread from outside the area of the fire.

▼ Grasses growing on the floor of a forest ravaged by fire in Montana in the USA in 1988.

Damaged plants may survive and regrow. Plants that need light grow well before tall trees shade the forest floor again. Shrubs and trees grow next. Animals return to eat the new plants. Animals that eat other animals come later.

Adapting to fire

Some plants and trees are well suited to surviving fires. Sequoia trees have thick, protective bark. Their high branches and deep roots are safe from surface fires. The aspen grows new shoots from any undamaged part. Some seeds lie in the ground until a fire warms them and sets them growing.

FIRE PINES

Fire pines such as the jack pine need fires to release their seeds. The seeds are in cones, held together by sticky **resin**. Fire melts the resin and lets out the seeds. Without fires, the fire pines would die out.

▲ This seedling of a jack pine has grown after fire opened the pine cone.

Forest Fires and **People**

Forest fires are very dangerous. Often, people see smoke and flames and can run away from a forest fire. But it is easy to be confused in the smoke, noise and heat and become trapped between flame fronts. People are often killed by smoke.

▼ A house surrounded by trees is at risk of burning in a forest fire near Marseilles in France.

Damage to buildings

Many people live near areas where forest fires are common. Often, their houses are made from wood. These easily catch fire if burning embers land on them or if the heat from the fire becomes very intense. It is not only houses that are lost. Roads can be blocked by smoke and falling trees. Power and communication lines are often brought down. After a serious fire, the soil may wash away and there may be mudslides. Mats and fast-growing plants can help keep the soil in place.

Economic costs

Large forests are grown to provide wood for building or making paper. When these forests dry out in a hot summer, fire spreads quickly. The trees cost a lot to replace, and money from selling wood is lost for several years. An area may also lose money if tourists cannot come to camp, walk and fish.

CASE STUDY

Cedar Fire, 2003

The Cedar Fire was started accidentally by hunters in California, USA, in October 2003. It spread quickly through **scrub**, driven by hot, dry winds. More than 100,000 hectares of land burned. Homes, buildings and bridges were destroyed and 14 people died. It was one of the worst fires in Californian history.

▲ These people in Kuala Lumpur, Malaysia, are wearing masks to protect their lungs from smoke coming from forest fires.

Fighting Forest Fires

If a fire is spotted early, it can often be stopped. When a fire is already going, firefighters work out how to control it. Their plan depends on the land, the fuel in the forest and the weather. They sometimes leave a fire to burn itself out if it is not dangerous.

Finding fires

During the fire season, people look out for smoke. Some places have lookout stations on hilltops. Fire rangers also watch the forest from the air and ground. If someone spots smoke, the fire has to be found. A plane with an **infrared scanner** measures where there is heat to find the fire.

▶ A photo from space shows a fire in Idaho, USA. A huge team of people, helicopters, bulldozers and fire engines fought the fire.

The fire-control team draws maps so that firefighters can move in by truck, on foot or by plane.

Attacking a fire

Firefighters use direct or indirect ways to fight a fire. They fight small fires directly. They spray water on the fire or cover it with earth or ash. They may rake the fuel away or beat the fire out.

Indirect firefighting stops fierce fires spreading. Firefighters may clear fuel ahead of the fire to make a **firebreak**. The fire cannot cross the firebreak. They may even light another fire in front of the main fire. This is called a back fire. It uses up the fuel. Firefighters may spray water or fire retardants on the fuel.

▲ Firefighters and soldiers make a firebreak to stop a fire from spreading.

 FIREBREAKS

A firebreak is a corridor through the forest where fuel has been cleared by firefighters. Rivers, roads, railways and lakes make natural firebreaks.

Firefighting Equipment

Forest firefighters use special equipment and work over a huge area. They have to make **firebreaks** and try to control flames.

Hand tools

Firefighters use hand tools to clear fuel. They use rakes to move burning material and beaters to beat down flames. They cut down trees with chainsaws and dig out roots with shovels. American firefighters use a special tool called a pulaski. It is like an axe and a hoe together. They use it to chop branches and scrape away **litter**.

Firefighters also carry safety equipment. They have fireproof suits and helmets. They carry special shelters like small tents with a metal covering. These keep them safe in **temperatures** of up to 315 degrees Celsius.

▼ A French firefighter sprays water onto a fire. It cools the fire and stops more fuel from burning.

Firefighting machines

Trucks carry firefighters and equipment to a fire. They take hoses and water pumps. They may carry water, or drag trailers with water tanks. Bulldozers are used to clear the ground. Aircraft drop firefighters near the fire and help to rescue people. Some aircraft scoop up water from lakes and drop it onto the fire. They sometimes mix fire-retardant chemicals into the water to stop the fuel from burning.

◄ Fire-retardant chemicals are dropped from a plane onto a fire in the south of France.

FIRE JUMPERS

Fire jumpers are the first to attack a fire in a remote area. They are dropped from planes with parachutes. They take firefighting equipment, food, water and first-aid equipment. Often, they can put out a fire just as it is starting.

Fire Warnings and **Protection**

▼ Fire beaters like these are used to beat out flames.

During the fire season, firefighters stay on standby and the authorities look out for fires all the time.

Weather and fuel

Portable weather stations in the forest keep track of **temperature** and **humidity** during the fire season. The risk of fire is highest when it is very hot and dry. Fire monitors watch the state of the fuel in the forest. Many fires are started by lightning. Systems on the ground monitor lightning strikes to help people work out where fires may start.

Predicting the spread

Scientists use computers to work out how a fire will spread once it has started. Firefighters can then plan how to fight the fire, and people are helped to leave dangerous areas.

Fire protection

If a fire comes near houses, people must protect themselves. They should wear cotton or wool clothing, gloves, goggles and a helmet. They should collect tubs of water and wet blankets to beat out flames. They must put out any small fires that start. Houses are less likely to burn if they are made of bricks and have clear space around them.

▲ A fire danger sign. There is a low risk if it has rained recently.

DANGER RATING

Many countries have a scale to show people how likely a fire is in their area. The information is put on the Internet and shown on notices in forests. The system in the USA has five levels of risk. They are shown on maps using different colours, from dark green for low risk to red for extreme risk.

Preventing Forest Fires

The best way to stop a fire is to prevent it from starting! We can't stop lightning, but we can try to stop fires from starting by accident.

Education

Fire-risk education programmes use school visits and adverts to tell people about risks. They try to stop people from starting fires by accident. Posters and signs near forests tell people about safe and unsafe behaviour.

Controlling campfires

Campfires often cause forest fires. Sometimes they get out of control, and sometimes people don't put them out properly. Campers should:

- Not start a fire in times of high risk.
- Make a bare patch of soil two metres across before lighting a fire.
- Light only a small fire.
- Dip used matches in water.
- Watch the fire all the time.
- Pour water on the fire and the ground around it before leaving.

▲ A forester lights a fire to clear the forest floor of litter and prevent more serious fires.

Forest management

Careful management of a forest can prevent fires. If there is a high risk of fires, the forest can be closed to visitors.

Forest managers sometimes set fire to forests on purpose. These are prescribed fires. They are kept under control so that they don't spread. They burn away **litter** that could be a fire risk.

▲ A child learns about firefighting in California, USA. Smokey Bear is in the background.

SMOKEY BEAR

The US Forest Service has a cartoon character called Smokey Bear as a mascot. Smokey Bear has been used since 1944 to help educate children about fire. Since the Smokey Bear campaign started, forest fire damage has been cut by three-quarters.

TEN OF THE DEADLIEST FOREST FIRES

When	Where	Casualties
1871	Peshtigo, Wisconsin, USA	1,200–2,000
1949	Cloquet, Minnesota / Wisconsin, USA	400–500
1894	Hinckley, Minnesota, USA	418
1881	Thumb, Michigan, USA	282
1987	North-east China	212
1825	Miramichi, New Brunswick, USA	160
1939	Victoria, Australia	76
1983	Victoria, Australia	71
1967	Hobart, Australia	62
2003	Portugal	18

GLOSSARY

carbon — A chemical element that is the main building block of all animals and plants.

convection — A movement of heat by air currents.

deciduous — Describes a tree that loses its leaves every year.

drought — A period of time when there is little or no rainfall.

firebreak — A strip of land that has been cleared of trees, bushes and other material in order to prevent a fire from spreading.

humidity — A measure of the amount of water vapour in the atmosphere.

infrared scanner — A device that detects infrared (heat) radiation.

litter — Fallen leaves, twigs and branches on the forest floor.

micro-organism — An animal or plant that is so small that it can only be seen through a microscope.

nutrient — A substance needed by plants and animals to live and grow.

oxygen — A chemical element that is found as a gas in the atmosphere.

radiation — A form of energy that travels in rays or waves. Heat, light and radio waves are types of radiation.

resin — A thick, sticky substance that leaks from trees.

scrub — An area of low, straggly vegetation.

slash-and-burn — Clearing land for farming by cutting down and burning forest.

temperature — A measure of how hot something is.

FURTHER INFORMATION

Books

The Atlas of the World's Worst Natural Disasters by Lesley Newson (Dorling Kindersley, 1998)

Awesome Forces of Nature: Blazing Bush and Forest Fires by Shaun McCarthy (Heinemann Library, 2003)

Fire and Flood by Nicola Barber (Ticktock Publishing, 1999)

Forest Fire by Douglas Dixon (Waterbird Books, 2005)

Websites

www.fs.fed.us/fire/

The wildfire section of the US Forest Service website.

www.smokeybear.com

The website of the Smokey Bear fire education programme.

www.fs.fed.us/fire/people/smokejumpers

All about smoke jumpers.

www.fs.fed.us/land/wfas/fd_class.gif

An up-to-date fire-danger map for the USA.

earthobservatory.nasa.gov/NaturalHazards

Select 'Fires' for satellite images of the latest forest fires.

INDEX

Page numbers in **bold** refer to illustrations.

accidental fires 5, 10, 21, 28
aircraft 22, 23, 25, **25**
animals 5, 17, **17**, 18, 19
ash 16, 18, 23
Australia 9, 10, 15, 30

back fires 23
beaters 23, 24, **26**
birds 17
blow-ups 15
bulldozers 25
bush fires 15

campfires 10, **10**, 28
carbon 7, **7**, 30
casualties 15, 21
Cedar Fire 21
chainsaws 24
China 30
crown fires 14, **14**, 16
Cyprus **12**

deciduous trees and forests 13, 30
deliberate fires 10, 11, **28**, 29
droughts 5, **8**, 9, 11, 15, 30

education programmes 28, 29
eucalyptus trees 13, 15, **15**
evacuations 26

fighting fires 7, 22–25, **29**
firebreaks 23, **23**, 24
fire danger rating systems 27, **27**
fire detection 22, 26
fire devils 15

firefighters 5, 7, 22, 23, **23**, 24, **24**, 25, 26
firefighting equipment 23, 24–25, **26**
fire jumpers 25
fire pines 19, **19**
fire prediction 26
fire protection 27
fire retardants 23, 25, **25**
fire season 9, 26
fire triangle 6, **6**, 7
fire trucks 25
fire warnings 26, 27
flame front 12, 20
forest floor 10, 13, 14, 15, **18**
forest management **28**, 29
forest soil 16, 17, 18
France 8, **8**, **20**, **24**, **25**
fuel 6, 7, 8, 12, 13, 22, 23, 25, 26

giant sequoia **5**, 19
grasses 13, 15, 18, **18**
grasslands 5, 13, **13**
ground fires 15, 16

hand tools 24
heat 6, 7, 8, 12, 20
human-made forest fires 5, 10–11, 28, **28**, **29**

Indonesia 11, **11**

land management 10
lightning 5, 9, **9**, 17, 26
litter 15, 24, 29, 30

Malaysia **21**
North America 8
nutrients 16, 30

oxygen 6, 7, 30

pioneer plants 18, 19
Portugal **15**, 30
property 11, 20, **20**, 21, 27
pulaskis 24

rain 9, 11, 17
rainforests 9, 11
regrowth 5, 18, 19
rescue 25

scrub 5, 21
shrubs 13, 15, 19
slash-and-burn 10, 11, **11**, 30
smoke 4, 5, 6, 7, 11, 17, **17**, 20, **21**, 22
Smokey Bear **27**, 29, **29**
succession 18
surface fires 15, 16, 19

USA **4**, 10, 11, **14**, 17, **17**, **18**, 21, **22**, **23**, 27, **27**, 29, **29**, 30

volcanic eruptions 9

water 6, 7, 23, **24**, 25, 27, 28, **29**
wind 12, **12**, 13, 14, 15, 21

Yellowstone National Park 17, **17**